Pachelbel's Canon
by Johann Pachelbel

arranged for harp solo, harp duet,
and harp and flute or violin

by

SYLVIA WOODS

Table of Contents

Key of D

Key of G

Artwork by Steve Duglas

©1986 and 1994 by Sylvia Woods, Woods Music and Books
Sylvia Woods Harp Center
P.O. Box 223434
Princeville HI 96722 USA

www.harpcenter.com

ISBN 0-936661-18-6

Notes From Sylvia Woods About The Arrangements:

The "Canon" by Johann Pachelbel has become one of the most requested classical pieces in recent years. It has been used in numerous commercials for items as diverse as wine and light bulbs. It was also the theme for the movie "Ordinary People". Because of its popularity for weddings and other occasions, it is an important piece for all harp players to have in their repertoire. This book contains several different versions of this famous piece.

Johann Pachelbel (1653-1706) was a German composer and organist. His organ fugues and chorale variations had a considerable influence on Bach. His most famous piece today is his "Canon and Gigue in D Major for 3 Violins and Basso Continuo", which has been arranged for a wide variety of solo and ensemble instruments.

You may wonder why I wrote this book in two parts, with the first half in the Key of D, and the second in the Key of G. The original key for this *Canon* was D. However, on many lever harps it sounds much better in the key of G. Another reason for the two keys is to accommodate harps with various ranges. For example, in the Key of D the "Easy Harp Solo" can be played on a small harp with a range of only one octave below middle C, and the "Advanced" versions need two octaves below middle C. In the Key of G, all the arrangements need a harp with a range going down 1½ octaves below middle C, to the G that is the bottom line on the bass staff.

Sharping lever changes for lever (non-pedal) harp players are indicated between the treble and bass clef staves. Pedal changes for pedal harpists are indicated below the bass clef.

What Is A Canon?

Here is how the "Oxford Junior Companion to Music" defines the word "canon".
When a piece of music is called a Canon it means that it obeys the rule of "Follow-my-leader". . . There are many different kinds of canon, some of which call for great ingenuity. . . Short vocal canons for singing are called rounds or catches. The idea behind the word "round" being that the melody comes "round" again and again, and that behind the word "catch" being that the singers "catch" up the melody one after the other.

In the rounds we sang as children, the second singer usually begins after the first singer has sung one, two, or four measures. For example, the second singer comes in after "Are you sleeping, are you sleeping", or in another tune after "Three blind mice, three blind mice", or after "Row, row, row your boat".

In Pachelbel's "Canon", the second voice comes in after 4 measures, or 8 chords. You do not get the clear sense of a "round" in the solo harp arrangements. To hear the "round", you need another instrument (or more). It can be clearly heard in recordings of the original string quartet version, with the various instruments coming in one after another (but always after 4 measures). In the duet and ensemble arrangements in this book you can hear the round as well, as the "B" harp part is 4 measures "behind" the "A" or flute parts. For example, the melody that the flute or "A" Harp plays in measure 13 is then echoed by the "B" harp in measure 17.

Pachelbel's Canon De-mystified

In order to more easily learn to play Pachelbel's "Canon" it is important to understand that the entire piece is made up of a series of eight left hand chords which repeat in the same order every 4 measures. Sometimes the eight chord notes are in different octaves in various sections, but the chords are still the same.

In the key of G, the eight chords are as follows: **G D E B C G C D**. They ALWAYS come in this order. Since it is very important that you learn the order of these chords, I have come up with a mnemonic device having to do with fast food at Carls' Jr. Restaurants to help you remember them. The first letter of each of the words is the order in which the chords will come. Memorize this sentence:
"**G**reat **D**anes **E**agerly **B**ite **C**arl's **G**ood **C**orn **D**ogs".

In the key of D, the eight chords are: **D A B F# G D G A**. Your helpful mnemonic sentence is :
"**D**on't **A**ll **B**ears **F**eel **G**ood **D**oing **G**reat **A**cts".

If you memorize the sentence that goes with the key you will be playing, you'll find it much easier to learn the left hand and know where you are in the chord progression.

Have fun!

Pachelbel's Canon
Easy Harp Solo - Key of D

Arranged by Sylvia Woods

Music by Johann Pachelbel

The lowest note in this version is the D that is 7 strings below middle C.

Pachelbel's Canon
Advanced Harp Solo - Key of D

Arranged by Sylvia Woods

Music by Johann Pachelbel

Pachelbel's Canon
"A" Part for Harp Duet - Key of D

Arranged by Sylvia Woods

Music by Johann Pachelbel

13

14

Pachelbel's Canon
"B" Part for Harp Duet or Ensemble - Key of D

Arranged by Sylvia Woods

Music by Johann Pachelbel

This part can be used with the "A" Duet Part on page 12 or the Melody Instrument Part on page 20.

18

19

Pachelbel's Canon
Melody Instrument Part - Key of D

Arranged by Sylvia Woods

Music by Johann Pachelbel

**This arrangement is for flute, violin, or other melody instrument.
It is to be used with the "B" Harp Part on page 16.**

This page may be photocopied without infringing upon copyright.

Pachelbel's Canon
Easy Harp Solo - Key of G

Arranged by Sylvia Woods

Music by Johann Pachelbel

24

F#

F♮

F#

Pachelbel's Canon
Advanced Harp Solo - Key of G

Arranged by Sylvia Woods

Music by Johann Pachelbel

28

Pachelbel's Canon
"A" Part for Harp Duet - Key of G

Arranged by Sylvia Woods

Music by Johann Pachelbel

Pachelbel's Canon
"B" Part for Harp Duet or Ensemble - Key of G

Arranged by Sylvia Woods

Music by Johann Pachelbel

This part can be used with the "A" Duet Part on page 30 or the Melody Instrument Part on page 38.

35

Pachelbel's Canon
Melody Instrument Part - Key of G

Arranged by Sylvia Woods

Music by Johann Pachelbel

**This arrangement is for flute, violin, or other melody instrument.
It is to be used with the "B" Harp Part on page 34.**

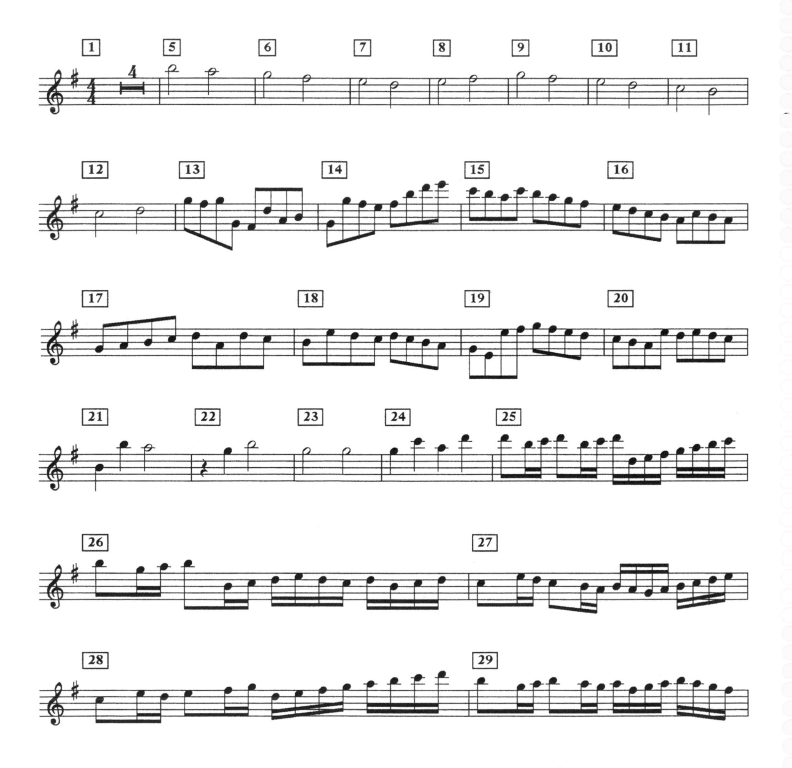

This page may be photocopied without infringing upon copyright.